O'Connell Street, Dublin. Nelson's Pillar and the General Post Office
O'Connell Street, Dublin. La colonne de Nelson et l'Hôtel des postes
O'Connell Street, Dublin. Nelson-Säule und Hauptpost

DUBLIN
AND CORK

A Book of Photographs by
R. S. MAGOWAN

With an Introduction by
KATE O'BRIEN

SPRING BOOKS · LONDON

Published by

SPRING BOOKS

SPRING HOUSE · SPRING PLACE · LONDON NW 5

© Books for Pleasure Ltd. 1961

Printed in Czechoslovakia

T 794

Also available in this series

LONDON

FLORENCE

ROME

PARIS

VENICE

OXFORD AND CAMBRIDGE

Contents

OBEDIENTIA·CIVIUM·URBIS·FELICITAS

THE ARMS OF THE CITY OF DUBLIN
LES ARMES DE LA CITE DE DUBLIN
WAPPEN DER STADT DUBLIN

Introduction

THERE is one accident of Ireland's appearance that gives it novelty, and a slightly foreign look in English or European eyes. That is — our time-lag. We always seem to keep a good few years behind the rest of the world in the things that show outward results — in the sciences, in mechanical and industrial progress; and in architecture, literature and the fine arts. This leisureliness has often shown itself to be no bad thing; and indeed, at this moment of time, when we consider the state of fuss, discomfort and restlessness into which an affluent society is getting itself almost everywhere else on the globe, some people are inclined to call the Irish time-lag a fruit of long-sighted wisdom. It is no such thing, of course; it is more likely an accident of history and temperament. But it is a happy accident, or so it will seem when you walk in peaceful contemplation round Dublin or Cork.

I showed these photographs to an English friend, a painter who knows Ireland well, who has often worked there and loves its whole ambience, as painter-material. She smiled affectionately at times, murmuring, 'How old-fashioned they look!'

I knew what she meant. These children, sitting in glorious eighteenth century doorways, or hanging over Liffey walls, or awaiting their turn at the Horse Show, do look old-fashioned in that they look truly shy, but also friendly, and a bit puzzled by the picture-taker's interest in them. Also, their clothes — though mostly quite good, for in Ireland too, thank God, we are eliminating the great savageries of poverty — they too look old-fashioned.

This slight out-of-stepness served the cities of Ireland well when in the fifties and sixties the social-climbing *bourgeoisie*, like its opposite numbers elsewhere, began to invent suburban life and to build itself fine villas round Dublin Bay and up amongst the little hills. Because in Ireland, right up to and beyond 1851 and the Great Exhibition of London which so perilously injured general English taste, we still thought in terms of Regency and late Georgian; and so we got those fine suburban houses, all stucco and wide windows and broad up-stepped porches — houses still superbly habitable and sympathetic — at a time when all the up-to-date world around us was inventing a new, alarming Gothic to live in, and even casting daring eyes at Tudor. And that piece of luck goes for Cork too, strongly, where there are still lovely suburbs; and for many of Ireland's smaller towns.

And the funny thing about this slowness of Ireland is that we reap advantage from it both ways. By the time we have begun to notice, in architecture say, that functionalism and stream-lining and so on are interesting, the rest of the world has cut its teeth on these ideas; burnt its fingers maybe — anyhow made a few of the major mistakes from which Ireland can, quite unfairly, profit. So that when our young architects — and we have some very good ones — are, after much humming and hawing, allowed to chance a twentieth century school, church or block of offices, they usually produce something striking, right and lovely. That really is true. Ireland, being poor, cannot rush into great spates of new building; and our important people, the tycoons who give the orders, are also strongly controlled by our native time-lag. But when a new building goes up now, usually — and I am averting my memory from one or two Cathedrals which the Hierarchy has imposed upon the island lately — usually we do get modern work that is truly fitting and to the point.

What is more, the building idiom of our time suits the Irish scene to a T. There is some felicity for Irish light

5

and weather in the materials that architects are using; and the austere lines of most modern buildings are sympathetic to our uncrowded, stony landscape, and to our clear skies. This sympathy of new buildings set down amidst the work of a century or two ago is very striking in rural Ireland; but both Dublin and Cork give us many happy evidences of it.

Looking at a picture of Dublin taken from the top of Nelson's Pillar, I exclaimed: 'What a country town it is after all!' For all around are hills and woods and the sea. It only accents and proves, of course, what Dubliners know and feel all day and night; the presence within walking distance of the city centre of sweet valleys, trout streams, high woods and sandy shores. Wherever one walks in Dublin, one cannot lift one's eyes to the end of the street without seeing blue hills or lapping water. This is perennially wonderful, when the streets are so wide and stately, so very much the streets of a capital city.

Not only are these lovely boundaries forever coming into sight, but in and out through this busy capital the Liffey meanders, under its many bridges, on its way out to the sea after it swirls past O'Connell Bridge and the glorious Custom House. The canal, too, skirts round the Georgian squares, swans, swimming boys, barking dogs and all; and St. Stephen's Green, an enchanting planned and planted public garden, full of the mingled pleasures of leafage and flowers and bird-and-water life, riotous with the flying games of children — with room too in its sunlight and shadow for the lonely pacings of young poets, young satirists and patriots, for the flirtations of university students, and for old men asleep — St. Stephen's Green gives the south side of this green-girdled town an unnecessary but lovely reminder of the nearby fields and streams. Ah no, not unnecessary; for the little children from neighbouring York Street, for instance — a Georgian slum just beyond its west gates — St. Stephen's Green is anything but unnecessary. It is a godsend, and well they know it.

And to the North of this country-town-capital there lies the Phoenix Park, a heavenly enclosure — and as vast and bountiful of variety of beauty and of occasions for pleasure as any heaven the ordinary imagination can invent. The President of Ireland, happy man, lives in the deep middle of this deep, green park. So does the American Ambassador, and so do all the young boys up from the country who are training to be Gardai — police. So do all the animals in a very charming zoo. You can play polo in this park, or watch the horses losing your money on an extremely pretty racecourse. You can listen to music, or you can merely walk, quite lost and at peace, watching young deer, watching birds; or you can sit on the grass and write a short story.

So Dublin is hedged about by green Nature, and not satisfied with that safeguard, has adapted rusticity into her impressive set-up of streets and bridges.

Cork, smaller than Dublin and entirely different in style, shares with the capital the good luck of a very beautiful setting. It is a harbour, to begin with, and a very active one, for Cork is a relatively rich city, commercially go-ahead and ambitious. Set down in a green valley between hills up which some of its streets run at a very fierce gradient, Cork is built not only all about the twistings and branchings of its 'own lovely Lee', but its very centre, wide Patrick Street, stretches right over a tributary of that river.

Certainly there is water everywhere in Cork, and the architecture, 18th, 19th and 20th century, sits easily against all the flowings and reflections of sea and stream. There are many birds, and parks, and bridges — and easy-going wide esplanades and quaysides where old men take their ease, market women argue and children go as they please. Indeed, although one knows Cork to have a forward-looking spirit and to be quicker in putting contemporary ideas into action than some other towns in Ireland, nevertheless when one is there one is enchanted by the easy pace, the soft speech. It is a gentle, well-mannered place; its people are handsome, especially the girls — handsome and well-dressed; and although there is a living gaiety, a sense of wit and quick thinking in the air, yet that air is very soft, and can be perilously inductive of the mood of *dolce far niente*. Indeed, I have yet to find the Irish town that is not generous of that old suggestion!

Cork must, for all its gaiety of face and manner, be very holy. Certainly it possesses a great number of churches and chapels, and many of these, both old and new, are of great beauty. For modern architecture has settled down very well in old Cork; and in nothing has the new idiom better adorned the city than in some of its new places of worship. For instance, high up on a northern hill in a new suburb called Spangle Hill, stands the new church of The Holy Trinity. The illustration in this book has caught dramatically the effect of the exquisite young spire, indeed all the calm and lonely grace, against the sky.

Tenderness, irony and awareness of contrast — these make up the real power of this book. Human figures are observed, in gaiety or weariness or meditation, in relation to inflexible stone or lapping water. Birds frequent the pages, as they do the streets of Dublin and of Cork; sunlight and the lamps of night throw sharp or gentle accents. There is a fine photograph of Dublin's Parnell monument, with an old, tired lady sitting below it — not reading Parnell's words at all; just sitting. It is a beautiful composition — full of Dublin. And among many fresh and stimulating views of Cork, how delightful it is to see that the lovely clock tower of St. Mary's, Shandon, has not been omitted.

Introduction

IL y a un aspect de l'Irlande qui la singularise et qui lui donne, aux yeux des Anglais ou des Européens un air un peu exotique : c'est son fameux retard. Il semble que nous ayons toujours quelques années de retard sur le reste du monde en ces matières où les résultats sautent aux yeux : en matière de sciences ou de technique, d'architecture, de littérature ou de beaux-arts. Pourtant cette sorte de lenteur n'est pas forcément une mauvaise chose ; et même, à considérer l'agitation désordonnée à laquelle les sociétés prospères sont livrées presque partout ailleurs, certains sont enclins à y voir le fruit d'une sage et clairvoyante philosophie. C'est plutôt, avouons-le, un accident de l'histoire et du caractère national. Mais c'est un heureux accident, comme vous le reconnaîtrez en vous promenant dans une pacifique contemplation par les rues de Dublin ou de Cork.

J'ai montré les images de ce livre à une amie anglaise, une artiste peintre qui connaît bien l'Irlande pour y avoir souvent travaillé, et en aime l'atmosphère éminemment pittoresque. Elle les a regardées, en souriant d'un air attendri : «Comme c'est vieux-jeu!», murmura-t-elle.

Je vois bien ce qu'elle voulait dire. Ces enfants, assis au pied de superbes portails du XVIIIème siècle, ou penchés sur le parapet des bords de la Liffey, ou faisant la queue pour entrer au Concours hippique ont en effet l'air d'un autre âge : foncièrement timides, mais en même temps gentils, et un peu effarés par l'intérêt que leur porte le photographe. Leurs vêtements aussi, bien que de bonne qualité le plus souvent, car en Irlande également, Dieu merci, nous faisons la chasse à l'odieuse misère, leurs vêtements ont l'air désuets.

Ce léger décalage dans le temps a été bénéfique pour les villes d'Irlande lorsqu'il y a environ un siècle, la bourgeoisie en plein essor, ici comme ailleurs, commença à inventer la banlieue et à se faire bâtir de belles villas le long de la baie de Dublin et parmi les collines qui entourent la ville. Car en Irlande, jusque et au delà même de 1851 et de la Grande Exposition de Londres qui pervertit si dangereusement le goût anglais, nous sommes restés attachés au style Régence et fin Georgien. C'est pourquoi nous avons ces belles résidences des alentours de Dublin, avec leurs moulures de stuc, leurs larges fenêtres et leurs nobles porches exhaussés — maisons encore très agréables à habiter de nos jours, alors que tous les gens à la page, à l'étranger, étaient en train d'inventer un nouveau, inquiétant Gothique, ou même s'aventuraient dans le Tudor. La même chance échut à Cork, dont la banlieue est restée délicieuse, et à plusieurs autres cités d'Irlande.

Ce qui est piquant, c'est, que grâce à cette fameuse lenteur irlandaise, nous gagnons sur les deux tableaux. Avant que nous ayons commencé à découvrir, en architecture par exemple, la valeur du fonctionnalisme ou du dépouillement des formes, le reste du monde s'est déjà acquis une large expérience, à ses dépens parfois, commettant quelques erreurs dont l'Irlande peut, fort injustement, profiter. De sorte que lorsque nos jeunes architectes — et nous en avons quelques-uns d'excellents — reçoivent, non sans peine certes, la commande d'une école, d'une église ou d'un immeuble administratif modernes, ils exécutent généralement quelque chose de remarquable à tous points de vue. C'est très vrai. L'Irlande est pauvre, elle ne peut construire avec prodigalité ; et nos autorités sont, elles aussi, des personnes qui retardent. Mais quand un nouvel édifice est construit de nos jours, en général — je passe sous silence une ou deux cathédrales que la Hiérarchie a imposées récemment — nous avons un ouvrage vraiment bien conçu et bien fait.

En plus de cela, le langage architectural de notre temps convient parfaitement au paysage irlandais. Il y a un certain bonheur dans le reflet de la lumière et du ciel irlandais sur les matériaux qu'utilise aujourd'hui l'architecte ; et les lignes austères de l'immeuble le plus moderne s'harmonisent bien à notre paysage granitique, parfois un peu désolé, et à nos ciels clairs. Cette harmonie du moderne et du XVIIIème ou du XIXème siècle est très frappante dans l'Irlande rurale ; mais Dublin et Cork nous en donnent maintes heureuses preuves.

En regardant une photo de Dublin prise du sommet de la colonne de Nelson, je me suis écriée : «Comme la ville est provinciale, quand on y songe!» Car tout autour ce ne sont que collines, bois et côtes. Cela ne fait que confirmer, certes, ce que les habitants de Dublin peuvent constater chaque jour, à savoir qu'à distance de marche du centre de la ville se trouvent de grasses vallées, des rivières à truites, de hautes fûtaies et des plages de sable. Quiconque se promène à Dublin ne peut lever les yeux vers l'autre bout de la rue sans apercevoir de vertes collines ou des rivages. Spectacle dont on ne se lasse pas, quand les rues sont si larges et si nobles, de vraies rues de capitale.

Non seulement l'on aperçoit de partout ces pittoresques alentours, mais encore la ville est traversée par les méandres de la Liffey, qui après avoir franchi les nombreux ponts de Dublin, s'éloigne vers la mer après une dernière boucle derrière O'Connell Bridge et le glorieux Hôtel des douanes. Le canal lui aussi, sert de décor aux squares georgiens, avec ses cygnes, ses jeunes baigneurs, ses chiens qui aboient ; et le parc St. Stéphane, jardin public magnifiquement dessiné et planté, plein des plaisirs mêlés du feuillage, des fleurs, des animaux aquatiques, tout bruyant des courses et des jeux des enfants, avec quelque place aussi, dans son soleil ou ses ombrages, pour les pas solitaires des jeunes poètes, des jeunes écrivains ou patriotes, pour les flirts des étudiants, et pour les vieillards endormis — le parc St. Stéphane donne à la partie sud de cette ville enceinte de verdure comme un rappel inutile, mais charmant des prés et des cours d'eau voisins. Inutile, non ; car pour les petits enfants de York Street, par exemple — une rue de taudis georgiens situés juste au delà de la porte de l'ouest, St. Stéphane est justement très utile. C'est une aubaine, et ils sont les derniers à l'ignorer.

Au nord de cette «capitale-chef-lieu de province», se trouve Phoenix Park jardin délicieux, aussi vaste et aussi plein de beauté, de variété et d'occasions de plaisirs que l'imagination peut le rêver. Le Président de la République, l'heureux homme, habite au milieu de ce beau jardin. L'Ambassadeur des Etats-Unis aussi, et tous les jeunes garçons qui se préparent à devenir Gardaï — c'est-à-dire membres de la police. Sans oublier tous les animaux d'un très joli zoo. On peut jouer au polo dans ce parc, et regarder courir les chevaux et s'envoler ses espoirs sur un très coquet hippodrome. On peut écouter de la musique, ou se contenter de marcher, dans une paix absolue, observant les oiseaux, les jeunes daims ; ou s'asseoir sur l'herbe et écrire une nouvelle.

Ainsi Dublin est bordée de verdure. Mais, non satisfaite de cette sécurité, elle a même adapté la rusticité dans son impressionnant réseau de rues et de ponts.

Cork, plus petite que Dublin et tout à fait différente de style, partage avec la capitale l'heureuse fortune d'un très joli décor naturel. C'est d'abord un port, et très actif car Cork est une ville riche, entreprenante et ambitieuse. Située dans une verte vallée, entre des collines que grimpent certaines de ces rues à des angles fantastiques, Cork n'est pas seulement bâtie parmi les boucles et les lacis de sa «douce Lee», mais encore son centre même, le large rue Patrick, enjambe un affluent de cette rivière.

Il y a de l'eau partout à Cork, et les édifices, XVIIIème, XIXème, XXème siècles, se reflètent dans les eaux miroitantes du fleuve et de la mer. Il y a beaucoup d'oiseaux, de parcs et de ponts, de larges esplanades pour les promeneurs et de quais où les vieillards prennent leurs aises, où les marchandes s'affairent et où les enfants jouent. Bien que Cork soit connue pour être entreprenante et plus prompte que d'autres à innover, elle ne nous enchante pas moins par son rythme un peu nonchalant et par la douceur du langage. C'est une ville polie, bien élevée ; ses habitants sont beaux, spécialement les filles, jolies et bien mises ; et quoiqu'il y ait une aimable gaieté, un esprit vif et spirituel dans l'air, cet air n'en est pas moins très tendre, et pourrait dangereusement inciter au *dolce far niente*. En vérité, je n'ai pas encore trouvé de ville irlandaise qui ne laisse cette impression.

Cork, malgré la gaieté de son aspect et de ses habitants, doit être une ville très sainte. Elle possède un grand nombre d'églises et de chapelles dont beaucoup, vieilles ou neuves, sont d'une grande beauté. Car l'architecture moderne s'est très bien adaptée ici; et nulle part mieux que dans ses édifices religieux. Par exemple, au sommet de la colline qui domine la ville au nord, Spangle Hill, s'élève l'église moderne de la Sainte Trinité. Le photographe a magnifiquement saisi l'impression que l'on reçoit de cet exquis clocher, de sa grâce tranquille et solitaire, se découpant dans le ciel.

Tendresse, ironie, sens des contrastes — telles sont les qualités qui font le prix de ce livre. Des figures humaines sont observées, gaies, lasses ou méditatives, sur un fond de vagues ou de rochers. Les oiseaux y sont présents, comme ils le sont dans les rues de Dublin et de Cork; le soleil et les lumières de la nuit jettent leurs feux, implacables ou tendres. Il y a une belle image du monument élévé à la mémoire de Parnell, au pied duquel l'on voit une vieille femme aux traits las, assise, adossée au monument, simplement assise. C'est une belle composition, tout à fait évocatrice de Dublin. Et parmi de nombreuses vues de Cork, neuves ou originales, quelle joie de constater que le délicieux clocher de Ste. Marie de Shandon n'a pas été oublié!

Einleitung

MIT den Augen Englands oder des Kontinents betrachtet, wirkt an Irland vor allem eines neu und fremdartig: das irische Schneckentempo. Sind wir Iren doch immer im Hintertreffen, wenn es um äußerlich sichtbare Erfolge geht, mag es sich nun um Fortschritte in der Wissenschaft, der Technik und Industrie handeln oder die Architektur, literarische und musische Neuerungen betreffen. Dabei ist diese Gemächlichkeit nicht durchweg von Übel, im Gegenteil: Wenn man bedenkt, wie sich eine wohlhabende Menschheit fast überall auf unserem Globus in Aufregungen, Ängste und Unruhen stürzt, so neigt mancher dazu, die irische Bummelei als den Stein der Weisen zu betrachten. Davon kann natürlich keine Rede sein. Es handelt sich hier um das Zusammentreffen von geschichtlichen Gegebenheiten und nationaler Veranlagung: ein glückliches Zusammentreffen, so scheint es, wenn man auf beschaulichem Rundgang Dublin oder Cork durchstreift.

Ich habe die vorliegenden Photographien einer englischen Freundin gezeigt. Sie ist Malerin und kennt Irland gut, hat oft hier gearbeitet und liebt die Landschaft sehr. Beim Anblick der Bilder lächelte sie zuweilen flüchtig und murmelte zärtlich: „Wie altmodisch sie doch aussehen!" Ich verstand genau, was sie damit sagen wollte. Diese Kinder, hier im prächtigen Rahmen alter Torbögen, dort über die Kaimauern des Liffey gelehnt, dann wieder beim Schlangestehen vor der Horse Show, machen in der Tat einen altmodischen Eindruck, wenn man echte Verlegenheit altmodisch nennen will. Dabei sind die Gesichter freundlich und spiegeln wohl auch ein wenig Erstaunen über das Interesse des Photo-Onkels. Selbst ihre übrigens durchaus ordentliche Kleidung — auch in Irland ist die bittere Armut zum Glück im Schwinden begriffen — wirkt ein wenig altmodisch.

Dieses Nicht-ganz-Schritt-Halten hat den irischen Städten gutgetan, als das aufstrebende Bürgertum in den fünfziger und sechziger Jahren gleich seinen Standesgenossen in anderen Ländern begann, die Vororte für sich zu entdecken und prächtige Villen in der Dubliner Bucht und dem umliegenden Hügelland zu bauen. In Irland dachte man nämlich bis zum Jahre 1851 und sogar noch nach der den englischen Geschmack ernstlich gefährdenden großen Londoner Ausstellung nur an den Stil, den die Regentschaft und die spätgeorgianische Epoche geprägt hatten. Auf diese Weise entstanden in Irland all die schönen Vorstadtvillen mit viel Stuck, großen Fenstern und breiten Freitreppen, Häuser, die auch heute noch äußerst wohnlich und sympathisch anmuten. Währenddessen richtete sich die moderne Welt ringsumher aufreizend neu und „gotisch" ein oder liebäugelte sogar heftig mit dem Tudor-Stil. Der gleichen glücklichen Rückständigkeit haben wir die schönen Vororte in Cork und vielen kleineren Städten Irlands zu verdanken.

Merkwürdigerweise profitieren wir Iren auf zweifache Art von unserem mangelnden Tempo. Bis wir zum Beispiel in der Architektur gemerkt haben, daß der Funktionalismus, die Stromlinie und so weiter ernstzunehmen sind, haben sich die Pioniere anderer Länder bereits die Zähne daran ausgebissen, vielleicht sogar die Finger daran verbrannt und in jedem Fall einige Kardinalfehler begangen, aus denen Irland dann ungerechterweise lernen kann. Wenn unsere jungen Architekten — und es sind einige sehr gute darunter — nach vielen Wenn und Aber endlich eine moderne Schule, Kirche oder einen Bürohaus-Block bauen dürfen, so wird meistens etwas auffallend Gelungenes, Richtiges und Ansprechendes daraus. Das sind keine leeren Worte. Irland kann sich als armes Land auch auf dem Bausektor keine großen Sprünge leisten. Außerdem sind unsere maßgeblichen

Leute, die die Aufträge erteilen, ebenfalls dem landesüblichen Schlendrian unterworfen. Wenn dann aber ein neues Gebäude entsteht, so ist es meistens, wenn man einmal von ein oder zwei Kathedralen absieht, die uns der Klerus jüngst beschert hat, durchaus modern, zweckentsprechend und wohlgelungen.

Im übrigen sind die modernen Bauelemente geradezu wie für den irischen Landschaftscharakter geschaffen. Das von den Architekten verwendete Material paßt sich den irischen Licht- und Wetterverhältnissen aufs glücklichste an, und die strenge Linie der Moderne harmoniert mit der steinigen, sparsam besiedelten Landschaft unter dem klaren Himmel. Dieses Miteinander von neu und alt ist besonders im ländlichen Irland auffallend. Aber auch in Dublin und Cork finden wir viele solcher ansprechenden Synthesen.

Als ich mir Dublin, von der Nelson-Säule gesehen, auf einem Photo betrachtete, rief ich unwillkürlich: „Wie ländlich diese Stadt trotz allem ist!" Ringsumher Hügel, Wälder und Meer, so weit das Auge reicht. Ich hatte damit nur das ausgesprochen, was Kopf und Herz der Dubliner erfüllt: die Allgegenwart lieblicher Täler, Forellenflüsse, hoher Wälder und sandiger Küsten. Man kann in Dublin nicht aufblicken, ohne am Ende einer Straße blaue Hügel oder plätschernde Wellen zu erblicken. Der Genuß ist um so dauerhafter, als die Straßen breit und stattlich wirken, ganz wie die einer richtigen Hauptstadt.

Aber nicht allein diese reizvollen Ausblicke erfreuen den Dubliner an jeder Ecke. Auch der Liffey-Fluß gehört dazu, der sich auf seinem Weg zum Meer unter vielen Brücken durch diese emsige Stadt an der O'Connell Bridge und dem berühmten Zollhaus vorbeischlängelt. Und um die Straßen und georgianischen Plätze schlingt der Kanal sein schimmerndes Band. Schwäne schaukeln sich auf seinen Wellen, Jungen tummeln sich in dem Naß, und bellende Hunde beleben das Ufer. Dann ist da Stephen's Green, der wundervoll angelegte öffentliche Park, lebendiger Reigen aus Blumen, Zweigen und Vögeln am Wasser; Kinder toben auf den Rasenflächen, und zwischen Schatten und Sonne suchen der junge Dichter, der Spötter, der Patriot einsame Wege. Studentenpärchen tuscheln, alte Männer nicken im Schlummer auf den Bänken ein. St. Stephen's Green bringt auch den südlichen Teilen dieser „Stadt im Grünen" die Nähe von Flüssen und Feldern in Erinnerung — freundliche, doch überflüssige Geste. Sage ich überflüssig? Nicht für die Kleinen aus der nahen York Street, einem georgianischen Slum-Viertel an der Westflanke Dublins. Für sie ist St. Stephen's ein wahres Geschenk des Himmels, und sie wissen es zu schätzen.

Im Norden dieser ländlichen Hauptstadt liegt der Phoenix Park, ein paradiesisches Fleckchen Erde, so weit, so lieblich und so reich an vielfältigen Vergnügungen, wie man sie sich schöner nicht erträumen könnte. Der Präsident von Irland, der Glückliche, wohnt inmitten dieses tiefen, dunklen Grüns, desgleichen der amerikanische Botschafter und all die jungen Leute, die vom Lande nach Dublin gekommen sind, um als „Gardai" — Polizei — ausgebildet zu werden. Auch die Tiere des reizend angelegten Zoos leben in diesem gesegneten Eiland. Man kann dort Polo spielen, man kann den Pferden auf einer besonders schön gelegenen Rennbahn zusehen und dabei sein Geld verlieren, man kann Musik hören oder allein wandern, ganz einsam und ruhevoll, man kann das junge Wild aufspüren und die Vögel beobachten. Man kann sich natürlich auch ins Gras setzen und eine Kurzgeschichte schreiben.

So schmiegt sich diese Stadt in die schützenden Arme der Natur und nimmt ihren rustikalen Charme mit hinein in das eindrucksvolle Bild ihrer Straßen und Brücken.

Cork ist kleiner als Dublin und von ganz anderem Schlag. Mit der Hauptstadt hat es den Vorteil einer bezaubernden Lage gemeinsam. Cork ist eine Hafenstadt, sogar eine sehr aktive; es verfügt über ansehnlichen Reichtum und entfaltet eine rege wirtschaftliche Tätigkeit. Es liegt in einem grünen Tal zwischen Hügeln, an denen sich die oftmals steilen Straßen hinaufwinden; in seinem Wachstum hat es sich nicht einmal durch die Krümmungen und Nebenarme seines geliebten Lee behindern lassen; sogar seine Hauptstraße, die breite Patrick Street, überquert einen Arm dieses Flusses.

Natürlich ist Wasser das beherrschende Element in Cork, dessen Architektur, zumeist aus dem 18.—20. Jahrhundert stammend, gleichsam mit den Strömungen und Lichtreflexen von Meer und Fluß eine Einheit bildet. Es gibt viele Vögel und Parks, Brücken, breite, bequeme Promenaden und Kais, an denen alte Männer ausruhen, Marktweiber schnattern und Kinder sich tummeln. Zwar weiß man, daß Cork vom Geist des Fortschritts beseelt ist und zeitgemäße Anregungen schneller aufgreift als andere irische Städte, doch nimmt diese Stadt, kaum daß man dort ist, durch ihre leichte Art, den sanften Redefluß ihrer Bewohner gefangen. Es ist eine gemäßigte, eine wohlerzogene Stadt; ihre Menschen, besonders die Mädchen, sind hübsch anzusehen und gut gekleidet; viel Fröhlichkeit liegt dort in der Luft, Witz und Schlagfertigkeit sprühen, und doch verführt die laue

Brise so sehr zum „süßen Nichtstun". Allerdings weiß ich kaum eine irische Stadt, die den Geist des „dolce far niente" nicht heraufbeschwören würde.

Trotz seiner frohsinnigen Grundstimmung und legeren Art scheint Cork eine sehr fromme Stadt zu sein. Es besitzt nämlich zahlreiche alte und moderne Kirchen und Kapellen, oft von großer Schönheit. Die moderne Architektur ist in dem alten Cork auf fruchtbaren Boden gefallen und hat vor allem in den Gotteshäusern ihren beredten und schönen Ausdruck gefunden. So erhebt sich auf einem Hügel im Norden der Stadt in dem neuen Vorort Spangle Hill die moderne Holy Trinity Church. Die Abbildung in diesem Buch hat den Kontrast des grazilen, schlanken Turmes gegen den Himmel in seiner ausgewogenen Ruhe und einsamen Anmut dramatisch eingefangen.

Liebevolle Hingabe, Ironie und ein geschärfter Sinn für Gegensätze bestimmen den Zauber dieses Buches. Es zeigt Menschen, fröhliche, müde und nachdenkliche, vor leblosem Stein oder schmeichelndem Wasser; Vögel, wie sie die Straßen von Dublin und Cork beleben, sind immer wiederkehrendes Motiv. Sonnenlicht und Lampenschein setzen harte oder sanfte Akzente. Ein schönes Photo vom Dubliner Parnell-Denkmal ist zu sehen, mit einer alten, müden Frau darunter, die nicht etwa Parnells Inschrift liest, sondern ganz einfach dasitzt: eine wundervolle Komposition, erfüllt von der Atmosphäre Dublins. Und unter den frischen, lebendigen Bildern von Cork entdecken wir zu unserem Entzücken auch den reizvollen Glockenturm von St. Mary's in Shandon.

THE ARMS OF THE CITY OF CORK
LES ARMES DE LA CITE DE CORK
WAPPEN DER STADT CORK

Index

DUBLIN

CORK

COLOUR PLATES

O'Connell Street, Dublin. Nelson's Pillar and the General Post Office, *frontispiece*
O'Connell Street, Dublin. La colonne de Nelson et l'Hôtel des postes, *frontispiece*
O'Connell Street, Dublin. Nelson-Säule und Hauptpost, *Titelbild*

Dublin. The Liffey, *facing p. 16*   The Custom House, Dublin, *facing p. 17*
Dublin. La Liffey, *en regard de la page 16*   L'Hôtel des douanes, Dublin, *en regard de la page 17*
Dublin. Der Liffey, *gegenüber der Seite 16*   Das Zollhaus, Dublin, *gegenüber der Seite 17*

Dublin. The Liffey
Dublin. La Liffey
Dublin. Der Liffey

The Custom House, Dublin
L'Hôtel des douanes, Dublin
Das Zollhaus, Dublin

Le fleuve

DUBLIN'S RIVER

Dublin am Liffey

Lamp standards, O'Connell Bridge
Lampadaires, O'Connell Bridge
Laternen auf der O'Connell Bridge

The width of O'Connell Bridge exceeds its length
O'Connell Bridge est plus large que long
Die O'Connell Bridge ist mehr breit als lang

Some derive profit from passers-by
Certains tentent la clientèle des touristes
Die Passanten sind für manche ein Geschäft

Others derive inspiration from the river scene
D'autres cherchent l'inspiration au bord du fleuve
Andere lassen sich von der Flußlandschaft inspirieren

19

Grattan Bridge, named after the famous orator, Henry Grattan
Grattan Bridge, qui doit son nom à Henry Grattan, célèbre orateur
Die Grattan Bridge, benannt nach dem berühmten Redner Henry Grattan

The Metal Bridge is the only one of the twelve bridges over the Liffey reserved for pedestrians only
Metal Bridge est le seul des douze ponts de la Liffey qui soit réservé aux piétons
Die Metal Bridge ist als einzige der zwölf über den Liffey führenden Brücken den Fußgängern vorbehalten

Work in progress – St. George's Quay
Travaux de déchargement, quai St. Georges
Bei der Arbeit – St. George's Quay

Work over for the day – City Quay
Fin de journée, quai de la Cité
Nach getaner Arbeit – City Quay

22

Anything stirring down below?
Qu'est-ce qu'on voit là-dessous?
Was tut sich denn da unten?

Can't see a thing . . .
Je ne vois rien . . .
Nichts zu sehen . . .

Cargo boat on the River Liffey
Un cargo sur la Liffey
Frachter auf dem Liffey

The Custom House, built by the English architect, James Gandon, is one of the noblest buildings in Dublin

L'Hôtel des douanes, bâti par l'architecte James Gandon, est l'un des plus beaux édifices de Dublin

Das Zollhaus, von dem englischen Architekten James Gandon erbaut, ist eines der würdigsten Gebäude in Dublin

The Custom House at night
L'Hôtel des douanes, la nuit
Das Zollhaus bei Nacht

Night view of River Liffey and Eden Quay
La Liffey et le quai Eden, vus de nuit
Blick auf den nächtlichen Liffey und den Eden Quay

An elegant flotilla
Une élégante flotille
Elegante Flottille

SOUTH OF THE LIFFEY

Au sud de la Liffey

Südlich des Liffey

The Bank of Ireland, College Green, is one of Dublin's finest classical buildings
La Banque d'Irlande, College Green, est l'un des plus beaux monuments classiques de Dublin
Die Bank von Irland auf dem College Green gehört zu den schönsten klassischen Bauten in Dublin

The East Front of the Bank of Ireland. The Bank was formerly the seat of the Irish House of Parliament
Façade orientale de la Banque d'Irlande. Ce palais fut autrefois le siège du Parlement irlandais
Die Ostseite der Bank von Irland. Die Bank war früher Sitz des irischen Parlaments

The City Hall in Dame Street, formerly the Royal Exchange, where O'Connell served as the first Catholic Mayor of Dublin
L'Hôtel de Ville, Dame Street, ancienne Bourse de commerce; O'Connell y fut le premier maire catholique du Dublin
Die Stadthalle in der Dame Street, früher königliche Börse und einstiger Amtssitz des ersten katholischen Bürgermeisters, O'Connell

Carved head of the Irish warrior-king Brian Boru, outside Church of Most
Holy Trinity

Tête sculptée du roi-soldat Brian Boru, devant l'église de la Très Sainte Trinit

Gemeißelter Kopf des irischen Königs Brian Boru an der Fassade der Churcl
of Most Holy Trinity

Church of Most Holy Trinity, formerly the Chapel Royal,
adjoining the Castle

L'église de la Très Sainte Trinité, contiguë au château

Church of Most Holy Trinity, früher die königliche Kapelle,
grenzt an das Schloß

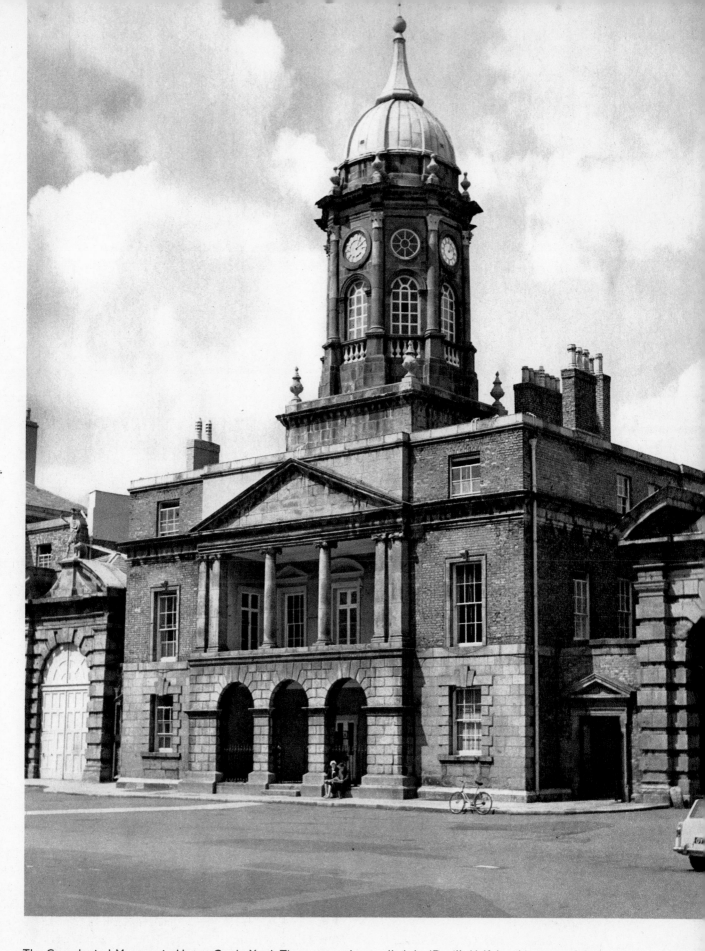

The Genealogical Museum in Upper Castle Yard. The courtyard was called the 'Devil's Half-Acre' because of the tortures which took place there in the rising of 1798

Le Musée généalogique dans Upper Castle Yard. Cette cour a été surnommée l'Arpent du Diable, en raison des tortures dont elle fut le théâtre durant le soulèvement de 1798

Das Genealogische Museum im oberen Schloßhof. Den Hof nannte man auch ‚Teufelsacker' wegen der Folterungen, die dort während des Aufstandes von 1798 stattfanden

The Record Tower of the Castle adjoins the former Chapel Royal. The Castle, built in the 13th century and twice rebuilt subsequently, was the residence of the Lords-Lieutenant of Ireland until 1922
La Tour des archives du château, à côté de l'ancienne Chapelle royale. Le château, érigé au XIIIème siècle et deux fois reconstruit depuis, fut la résidence des Lords-lieutenants d'Irlande jusqu'en 1922
Der Record Tower des Schloßes steht neben der früheren königlichen Kapelle. Das Schloß wurde im 13. Jahrhundert erbaut und seither zweimal wiedererrichtet; bis 1922 war es Residenz der irischen Vizekönige

Christ Church Cathedral, one of the two Dublin cathedrals, both of them Protestant. It was begun by the Normans on the site of an earlier Danish church
La cathédrale Christ Church, l'une des deux cathédrales de Dublin, toutes deux protestantes. Sa construction fut enterprise par les Normands sur l'emplacement d'une ancienne église danoise
Christ Church Cathedral, eine der beiden (übrigens protestantischen) Kathedralen Irlands. Sie wurde von den Normannen auf den Grundmauern einer früheren dänischen Kirche errichtet

The crypt of Christ Church may date back to the time of the Danish founder, Sigtryg, King of Dublin
La crypte de Christ Church date peut-être de l'époque du fondateur danois Sigtryg, roi de Dublin
38 Die Krypta der Christ Church wurde vermutlich von dem Dänen König Sigtryg von Dublin gestiftet

A covered archway in Winetavern Street links Christ Church Cathedral with the Synod House
Une arche couverte, rue de la Taverne, relie la cathédrale à Synod House
Ein überdachter Bogengang in der Winetavern Street verbindet Christ Church Cathedral mit der Synode 39

Ruins of the original St. Audoen's Church, one of the most ancient in Dublin
La vieille église St. Audoin, l'une des plus anciennes de Dublin
Die Ruine der alten St. Audoen's Church, eine der ältesten Kirchen Dublins

The modern Roman Catholic Church of St. Audoen's, adjoining the earlier church
La nouvelle église catholique St. Audoin, construite à côté de l'ancienne
An die ältere Kirche schließt sich die neue katholische St. Audoen's Church an

DEO.OPTIMO.MAXIMO.SVB.INVOC.S.AVDOENI.

Coopering yard, Guinness Brewery. The brewery is one of the oldest in the world and is one of Dublin's most thriving industries
Cour d'entonnage, la Brasserie Guinness. Cette brasserie est l'une des plus vieilles du monde, et l'une des grandes enterprises de Dublin
Faßlager in der Guinness-Brauerei; sie gehört zu den ältesten Brauereien der Welt und ist einer der wichtigsten Industriebetriebe Dublins

Modern canteen on the 600 acre site of the Guinness Brewery. The brewery is open every weekday to visitors

Cantine moderne à la Brasserie Guinness. Cette brasserie, qui occupe 240 hectares, est ouverte aux visiteurs toute la semaine

Moderne Kantine auf dem 240 Hektar umfassenden Gelände der Guinness-Brauerei. Die Brauerei ist wochentags für Besucher geöffnet

St. Patrick's Cathedral dates from the 13th century. Jonathan Swift was Dean from 1713–1745
La cathédrale St. Patrick date du XIIIème siècle. Jonathan Swift en fut doyen de 1713 à 1745
St. Patrick's Cathedral geht auf das 13. Jahrhundert zurück; Jonathan Swift war dort von 1713–1745 Dekan

Interior of St. Patrick's. The flags are of the Irish regiments and the Knights of St. Patrick
Intérieur de St. Patrick. Les drapeaux sont ceux des régiments irlandais et des chevaliers de St. Patrick
Innenansicht von St. Patrick's Cathedral mit den Fahnen der irischen Regimenter und der Ritter von St. Patrick

45

The Boyle Monument in St. Patrick's was erected by Richard Boyle, Earl of Cork, to commemorate his wife and 16 children. In the foreground is a statue to Captain Boyd of H.M.S. *Ajax*

Le monument Boyle, à St. Patrick, fut érigé par Richard Boyle, comte de Cork, en mémoire de sa femme et de ses 16 enfants. Au premier plan, une statue du Capitaine Boyd, commandant le H.M.S. *Ajax*

Boyle-Denkmal in St. Patrick's Cathedral; wurde von Richard Boyle, dem Grafen von Cork, zum Gedächtnis seiner Frau und seiner 16 Kinder errichtet. Im Vordergrund eine Statue des Kapitän Boyd von der H.M.S. *Ajax*

Monuments to Ireland's illustrious men in St. Patrick's. The second on the left portrays George Nugent Temple Greville, Lord-Lieutenant under Rockingham

Monuments dédiés aux Irlandais illustres, à St. Patrick. La deuxième statue à partir de la gauche est celle de George Nugent Temple Greville, Lord-Lieutenant au temps de Rockingham

Standbilder berühmter Iren in St. Patrick's Cathedral. Das zweite von links stellt George Nugent Temple Greville, Vizekönig unter Rockingham, dar

Creation Arcade, off Dublin's main shopping thorough-
fare, Grafton Street

Création Arcade, dans Grafton Street, principale rue
commerçante de Dublin

Creation Arcade, nahe Grafton Street, der Haupt-
geschäftsstraße von Dublin

Sunshine and summer flowers in a Dublin street
Soleil d'été, paniers fleuris dans une rue de Dublin
Sonnenschein und Sommerblumen in einer Straße Dublins

Children at play in York Street
Jeux d'enfants dans York Street
Kinder beim Spiel in der York Street

Bashful trio
Les trois timides
Schüchternes Trio

Confident couple
Main dans la main
Ein zuversichtliches Pärchen

Gay sextet
Un joyeux sextuor
Fröhliches Sextett

51

Mansion House, in Dawson Street, is the traditional home of Dublin's Lord Mayors
Mansion House, Dawson Street, est la résidence traditionelle des Lords Maires de Dublin
Mansion House, in der Dawson Street, traditioneller Sitz des Oberbürgermeisters von Dublin

The Carmelite Church of St. Teresa, off Grafton Street
L'église carmélite St. Thérèse, non loin de Grafton Street
Die Karmeliterkirche St. Teresa, in unmittelbarer Nähe der Grafton Street

St. Stephen's Green, transformed into a public park in 1880
St. Stephen's Green, devenu parc public en 1880
St. Stephen's Green, seit 1880 öffentlicher Park

St. Stephen's Green: in Dublin's fair city, the girls really are pretty
St. Stephen's Green: les jolies filles de Dublin
St. Stephen's Green: in der schönen Stadt Dublin gibt es wirklich hübsche Mädchen

St. Stephen's Green: critical public
St. Stephen's Green: un public difficile
St. Stephen's Green: kritische Besucher

St. Stephen's Green: optimistic artist
St. Stephen's Green: un artiste optimiste
St. Stephen's Green: optimistischer Künstler

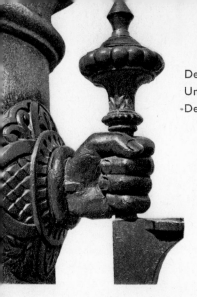

Detail, iron gate at entrance to University College
University College, détail de la porte principale
Detail der eisernen Eingangspforte zum University College

University College, with the colleges of Cork and Galway, constitutes part
of the National University of Ireland

University College, avec les collèges de Cork et de Galway, fait partie de
l'Université nationale d'Irlande

Das University College gehört mit den Colleges in Cork und Galway zur
irischen Universität, der National University of Ireland

The National Library, opposite the Museum, owns about half a million books and numerous manuscripts
La Bibliothèque nationale, face au musée, compte environ 500.000 livres et de nombreux manuscrits
Die Nationalbibliothek gegenüber dem Museum enthält etwa 500.000 Bücher und zahlreiche Handschriften

The National Museum in Kildare Street contains a priceless collection of Irish antiquities and other treasures
Le Musée national, Kildare Street, contient une collection inestimable d'antiquités irlandaises et d'autres trésors
Das Nationalmuseum in der Kildare Street beherbergt eine einzigartige Sammlung irischer Kunstgegenstände und andere wertvolle Stücke

The National Gallery, next to Leinster House, is particularly noteworthy for its excellent collection of Dutch masters
La Galerie nationale, près de Leinster House, est particulièrement célèbre pour sa très belle collection de maîtres hollandais
Die National Gallery neben dem Leinster House ist besonders wegen ihrer hervorragenden Sammlung holländischer Meister berühmt

Leinster House, once the focal point of fashionable Dublin life, is today the meeting place of the Dáil Éireann – the parliament of Ireland
Leinster House, autrefois le centre de la vie mondaine à Dublin, est aujourd'hui le siège de Dáil Éireann – le Parlement irlandais
Im Leinster House, dem einstigen Mittelpunkt der eleganten Welt von Dublin, tagt heute das Dáil Éireann, das irische Parlament

The College of Science, behind the Government buildings, forms part of the National University
Le Collège des sciences, derrière le palais du Gouvernement, fait partie de l'Université nationale
Das College of Science der National University liegt hinter dem Regierungsgebäude

Government buildings, Merrion Street, where all the main departments are accommodated
Le quartier administratif, Merrion Street, où sont groupés tous les grands ministères
Regierungsgebäude in der Merrion Street; dort sind die wichtigsten Ministerien untergebracht

A typical Georgian doorway in Merrion Square
Une belle porte de style georgien, Merrion Square
Ein rein georgianischer Eingang am Merrion Square

St. Andrew's Protestant Church in St. Andrew's Street
L'église protestante St. Andrew, dans St. Andrew's Street
Die protestantische St. Andrew's Church in der St. Andrew's Street

Trinity College, known simply as T.C.D., was founded in 1591. The main front facing College Green was built in 1752–1791

Trinity College, familièrement T.C.D., a été fondé en 1591. La façade principale, devant College Green, a été construite de 1752 à 1791

Trinity College, gewöhnlich T.C.D. genannt, wurde im Jahre 1591 gegründet. Die Vorderfront gegenüber dem College Green stammt aus den Jahren zwischen 1752 und 1791

Foley's statue of Oliver Goldsmith, together with that of Edmund Burke, stands by the main gateway of Trinity College. Both men were students here

A l'entrée de Trinity College se trouvent deux statues, bâties par Foley, d'anciens étudiants, Oliver Goldsmith et Edmund Burke

Das von Foley geschaffene Standbild Oliver Goldsmiths mit dem Edmund Burkes den Haupteingang zum Trinity College. Beide Männer haben hier studiert

Parliament Square, main quadrangle of Trinity College, with (left) the Chapel and (right) the Campanile
Parliament Square, cour principale de Trinity College. À gauche, la chapelle; à droite, le Campanile
Parliament Square, Hauptplatz des Trinity College; links die Kapelle, rechts der Glockenturm

Trinity College Chapel
La chapelle de Trinity College
Kapelle des Trinity College

Trinity College Examination Hall, similar in style to the Chapel
La salle d'examen de Trinity College, conçue dans le même style que la chapelle
Prüfungssaal des Trinity College: der Stil ähnelt dem der Kapelle

Roof of Examination Hall: the organ case was captured in a naval action off the coast of Spain in 1703

Le plafond de la salle d'examen : l'orgue a été rapporté d'une opération navale sur les côtes d'Espagne en 1703

Deckengewölbe des Prüfungssaal: die Orgel wurde 1703 in einem Seegefecht vor der spanischen Küste erbeutet

Monument in Examination Hall to Dr Richard Baldwin, a former Provost

La salle d'examen, monument à la mémoire de Dr Richard Baldwin, ancien Provost

Denkmal im Prüfungssaal für Dr Richard Baldwin, einstigen Leiter des Trinity College

71

Trinity College Museum: the Venetian-style entrance hall
Le musée de Trinity College : l'entrée, de style vénitien
Das Museum des Trinity College: Eingangshalle im venezianischen Stil

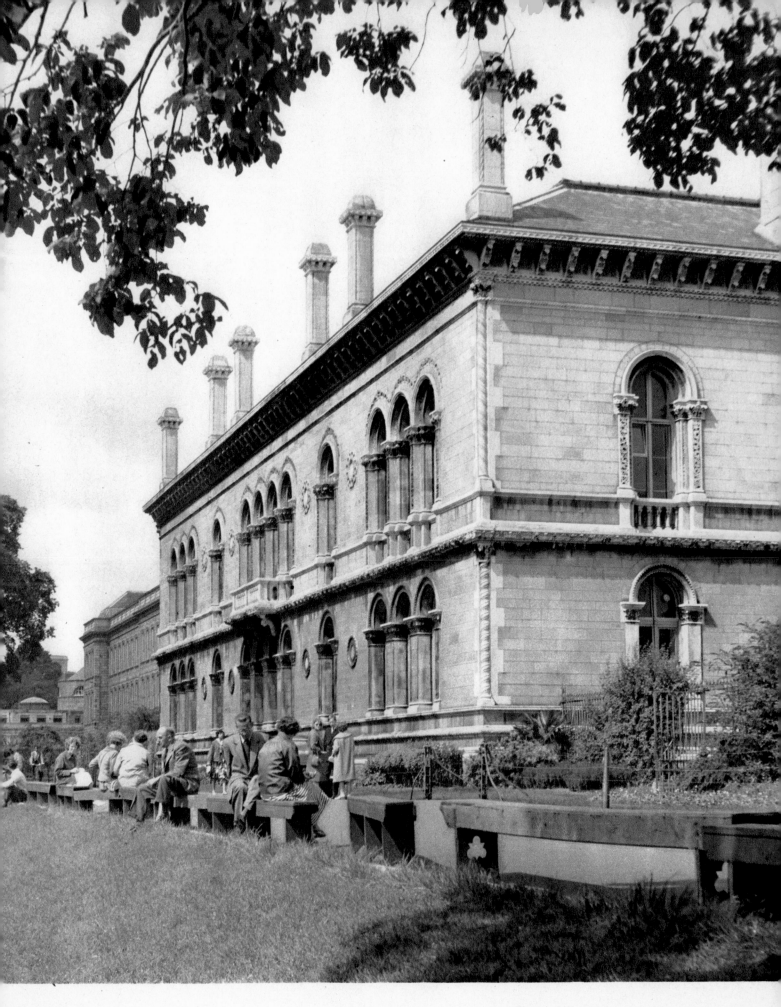

Trinity College Museum in New Square
Le musée de Trinity College, New Square
Das Museum des Trinity College am New Square

Trinity College Library contains the priceless Book of Kells, a 7th century illuminated copy of the Gospels

La bibliothèque de Trinity College contient le fameux Livre de Kells, exemplaire enluminé de l'Evangile datant du VIIème siècle

Die Bibliothek des Trinity College enthält das kostbare ,Buch von Kells', ein mit Buchmalereien geschmücktes Evangeliar aus dem 7. Jahrhundert

O'Connell Street, with the Wicklow Hills in the background, seen from the top of Nelson's Pillar
O'Connell Street, vue du sommet de la colonne de Nelson; au fond les collines de Wicklow
Blick von der Nelson-Säule auf O'Connell Street mit den Hügeln von Wicklow im Hintergrund

Au nord de la Liffey

NORTH OF THE LIFFEY

Nördlich des Liffey

O'Connell Street, one of the widest thoroughfares in Europe, looking towards O'Connell Bridge
O'Connell Street, l'un des plus larges carrefours d'Europe, dans le prolongement d'O'Connell Bridge
O'Connell Street, eine der breitesten Geschäftsstraßen Europas, mit Blick auf die O'Connell Bridge

O'Connell Street in gloomier garb
O'Connell Street, par un jour de pluie
O'Connell Street in unfreundlicherem Gewand

O'Connell Street: statue by Foley of Daniel O'Connell, leader of Catholic emancipation, known as the Liberator
O'Connell Street : statue bâtie par Foley de Daniel O'Connell, chef de l'émancipation catholique, surnommé le Libérateur
O'Connell Street: ein von Foley geschaffenes Standbild des ‚Befreiers' Daniel O'Connell, des Führers der katholischen Emanzipation

O'Connell Street: statues of William Smith O'Brien and Sir John Gray, the latter the founder of Dublin's water supply
O'Connell Street : statues de William Smith O'Brien et de Sir John Gray, ce dernier, fondateur du système d'adduction d'eau de la ville
O'Connell Street: Denkmäler von William Smith O'Brien und Sir John Gray, auf den Dublins Wasserversorgungsnetz zurückgeht

O'Connell Street: Nelson's Pillar and the General Post Office. The latter was the rebel headquarters during the Easter rising of 1916. It was destroyed by shellfire and the rebel leaders executed

O'Connell Street : la colonne de Nelson et l'Hôtel des postes. C'est ici que les rebelles tinrent leur quartier général durant le soulèvement du printemps 1916. L'édifice fut bombardé et les chefs rebelles exécutés

O'Connell Street: Nelson-Säule und Hauptpost. Das Postgebäude diente den Rebellen während des Oster-Aufstandes im Jahre 1916 als Hauptquartier. Es wurde durch Granatfeuer zerstört, die Rebellenführer wurden hingerichtet

Statues on roof of General Post Office, with Nelson's Pillar in background
Statues sur le toit de l'Hôtel des postes; au loin, la colonne de Nelson
Statuen auf dem Dach der Hauptpost, im Hintergrund die Nelson-Säule

Statue of Cuchullain in the central hall of the General Post Office, in memory of the men
who died in 1916

Statue de Cuchullain dans le hall de l'Hôtel des postes, érigée en mémoire des héros
de 1916

Standbild von Cuchullain in Hauptraum der Post, zur Erinnerung an die Toten von 1916

Dublin character
Personnage de Dublin
Dubliner Original

Selling football supporters' badges
Vente d'écussons aux supporters de football
Abzeichen für Fußballfans – wer unterstüzt wen?

Bookstall, Lower Liffey Street
A l'étal du bouquiniste, Lower Liffey Street
Bücherstand an der unteren Liffey Street

Guinness delivery, Marlborough Street
Livraison de bière, Marlborough Street
Guinness-Lieferwagen in der Marlborough Street

O'Connell Street: statue of Father Theobald Mathew, the monk who led a 19th century campaign against drunkenness and vice

O'Connell Street : statue du Père Théobald Mathew, le moine qui, au siècle dernier, fit campagne contre le vice et l'alcool

O'Connell Street: das Standbild des Pater Theobald Mathew, der im 19. Jahrhundert einen Feldzug gegen Trunksucht und andere Laster führte

FATHER
MATHEW
THE APOSTLE
OF
TEMPERANCE
CENTENARY STATUE
1890

The Rotunda Hospital, oldest maternity hospital in the British Isles, designed by the German architect Cassels
Rotunda Hospital, la plus ancienne maternité des Iles Britanniques, bâti par l'architecte allemand Cassels
Rotunda Hospital, das älteste Entbindungsheim auf den Britischen Inseln, von einem deutschen Architekten namens Cassels entworfen

The Rotunda assembly rooms now accommodate the celebrated Gate Theatre
Les salles de réunion de la Rotonde abritent aujourd'hui le fameux Gate Theatre
In die Empfangsräume der ‚Rotunda' ist heute das berühmte Gate-Theater eingezogen

Statue of Charles Stewart Parnell, the great Irish Nationalist leader
Statue de Charles Stewart Parnell, l'illustre nationaliste irlandais
Denkmal Charles Stewart Parnells, des großen irischen Nationalhelden

Panorama from Nelson's Pillar, showing, from left to right, the spires of St. Patrick's Cathedral, Christ Church Cathedral, Church of St. John the Baptist, and the dome of the Four Courts

Panorama de la ville, pris de la colonne Nelson. De gauche à droite : les clochers de St. Patrick, de Christ Church, de St. Jean Baptiste et le dôme des Quatre Cours

Aussicht von der Nelson-Säule: von links nach rechts die Türme der St. Patrick's Cathedral, der Christ Church Cathedral, der Kirche St. John the Baptist und die Kuppel der Four Courts

Marlborough Street. Nearby stood the famous Abbey Theatre, destroyed by fire in 1951

Marlborough Street. Non loin de là se trouvait le célèbre Abbey Theatre, détruit par un incendie en 1951

Marlborough Street. In der Nähe befand sich das berühmte Abbey-Theater, das 1951 durch Feuer zerstört wurde

St. George's Church, Hardwick Crescent, one of the most elegant churches in the city
L'église St. Georges, Hardwick Crescent, l'une des plus élégantes églises de la ville
St. George's Church, Hardwick Crescent, eine der elegantesten Kirchen der Stadt

The Presbyterian Church, Parnell Square, with its lofty spire
L'église presbytérienne de Parnell Square, et son fier clocher
Die presbyterianische Kirche am Parnell Square mit ihrem schlanken Turm

Church of the Holy Child, Swords Road
Eglise du Saint Enfant, Swords Road
Church of the Holy Child, Swords Road

Georgian doorway, Granby Row
Porte de style georgien, Granby Row
Georgianisches Portal in der Granby Row

The Busáras, or bus station: the building also houses the offices of the Department of Social Welfare

Le Busáras, gare des autobus : ce bâtiment abrite aussi les services du Ministère de la prévoyance sociale

Busáras, der Autobus-Bahnhof: in dem Gebäude ist auch das Sozialministerium untergebracht

Modern statuary in Marlborough Street school gardens
Sculptures modernes dans les jardins de l'école, Marlborough Street
Moderne Plastiken in den Schulgärten der Marlborough Street

95

Modern flats, Lower Gardiner Street
Appartements modernes, Lower Gardiner Street
Moderne Wohnungen in der unteren Gardiner Street

Modern flats, Railway Street and Beaver Street
Appartements modernes, Railway et Beaver Street
Moderne Wohnungen in der Railway Street und der Beaver Street

Sheep in the street
Un troupeau de moutons
Schafe auf der Straße

Cattle in the street
Bétail dans la rue
Vieh auf der Straße

Custom House
Hôtel des douanes
Das Zollhaus

St. Michan's Church, dating from the 17th century. In its vaults lie bodies which have not decayed, owing to some preservative quality in the air

L'église St. Michan, qui date du XVIIème siècle. Les corps que renferment les caveaux sont restés intacts en raison d'une qualité particulière de l'air, qui les conserve

St. Michan's Church aus dem 17. Jahrhundert. In den Grabkammern dieser Kirche liegen unverweste Leichen, durch einen bestimmten, in der Luft enthaltenen Wirkstoff konserviert

100

The Four Courts, housing the central courts of justice. This magnificent building was damaged in 1922 and restored from the original plans

Les Quatres Cours, où se trouvent les jurisdictions centrales. Ce magnifique palais, endommagé en 1922, a été restauré suivant les plans originaux

The Four Courts, Sitz des obersten Gerichtshofes. Der prächtige Bau fiel 1922 der Zerstörung anheim und wurde nach alten Plänen rekonstruiert

St. Peter's Roman Catholic Church, Phibsborough, has the highest spire in Dublin
L'église catholique Saint Pierre, Phibsborough, a le plus haut clocher de Dublin
Die katholische St. Peter's Church, Phibsborough, hat den höchsten Turm in Dublin

The Royal Canal virtually defines Dublin's northern limits, as does the Grand Canal in the south
Le Canal royal limite Dublin au nord, comme le fait le grand Canal au sud
Der Royal Canal begrenzt Dublin im Norden, so wie der Grand Canal im Süden

All Ireland Polo Club, Phoenix Park

Cricket, Phoenix Park

Finish of Tour of Ireland cycle race, Phoenix Park
Arrivée du Tour d'Irlande cycliste à Phoenix Park
Am Ziel: Radrennen ‚Tour of Ireland', Phoenix Park

The Wellington Monument in Phoenix Park, an unmistakable landmark
Le célèbre monument érigé à la mémoire de Wellington, à Phoenix Park
Das Wellington-Denkmal im Phoenix Park, ein unverkennbares Wahrzeichen der Stadt

Detail, Wellington Monument
Monument Wellington : un détail
Wellington-Denkmal: Ausschnitt

The Irish also have their bagpipes
Les Irlandais ont aussi leurs cornemuses
Auch die Iren haben ihren Dudelsack

Phoenix Park, People's Gardens: statue of Sean Heuston, revolutionary leader

Les jardins du peuple à Phoenix Park : statue de Sean Heuston, chef de la révolution

Phoenix Park, Volksgarten: Denkmal von Sean Heuston, dem Rebelenführer

Phoenix Park Zoological Gardens. The zoo was founded in 1830 and is the third oldest in the world
Le jardin zoologique de Phoenix Park a été fondé en 1830. C'est l'un des trois plus anciens du monde
Der Zoo im Phoenix Park wurde 1830 gegründet und ist der drittälteste der Welt

Bandstand in Phoenix Park. Extending over 1750 acres, this is the largest public park in Europe
Kiosque à musique, dans Phoenix Park. D'une superficie de 700 hectares, ce parc est l'un des plus vastes d'Europe
Orchesterpavillon im Phoenix Park, der mit einer Ausdehnung von 700 Hektar eine der größten öffentlichen Anlagen Europas ist

Hill of Howth, with Wicklow Hills in distance
Colline de Howth : au loin les Wicklow Hills
Hill of Howth, in der Ferne die Wicklow Hills

Autour de Dublin   *Umgebung von Dublin*

AROUND DUBLIN

Howth, some miles north of the capital, is a pleasant summer resort
Howth, à quelques kilomètres au nord de la capitale, est une agréable villégiature d'été
Howth ist ein erholsamer Ferienort einige Meilen nördlich der Hauptstadt

The lighthouse, Howth
Le phare de Howth
Der Leuchtturm von Howth

Dublin Airport is situated at Collinstown, north of the city. The buildings are spacious and imaginatively designed
L'aéroport de Dublin est situé à Collinstown, au nord de la ville. Ces vastes bâtiments sont construits dans un style très moderne
Der Flughafen von Dublin liegt im Norden der Stadt in Collinstown. Die geräumigen Gebäude sind phantasievoll entworfen

Howth Harbour
Le port de Howth
Der Hafen von Howth

Dublin Airport handles all the cross-channel and European traffic

L'aéroport, point de départ des services vers la Grande Bretagne et l'Europe

Der gesamte Verkehr nach Großbritannien und Europa läuft über den Flughafen von Dublin

Dublin Horse Show, Ballsbridge. The well-known horseman David Broome makes a winner's circuit
Le concours hippique de Dublin, à Ballsbridge. Le fameux cavalier David Broome en action
Dublin Horse Show, Ballsbridge. Der bekannte Reiter David Broome reitet als Sieger eine Ehrenrunde

Dublin Horse Show. Never too early to start . . .
Concours hippique. Il n'est jamais trop tôt pour commencer . .
Dublin Horse Show. Man kann nicht früh genug anfangen . . .

. . . whether spectator . . .
. . . qu'on soit spectateur . . .
. . . ob als Zuschauer . . .

... or aspiring competitor
... ou futur concurrent
... oder als angehender Reiter

Dublin Horse Show. This annual event attracts many visitors
Le Concours hippique de Dublin. Cette épreuve annuelle attire de nombreux visiteurs
Dublin Horse Show. Das alljährliche Ereignis lockt viele Besucher herbei

Trade Exhibition held during Dublin Horse Show
Foire commerciale durant le Concours hippique de Dublin
Messe während der Dublin Horse Show

Dun Laoghaire, with its fine artificial harbour, runs a regular cross-channel service with Holyhead
Dun Laoghaire, avec son beau port artificiel, est le point de départ d'un service régulier vers Holyhead
Dun Laoghaire mit seinem gut angelegten Hafen unterhält einem regelmäßigen Verkehr über den Kanal nach Holyhead

Dun Laoghaire, seven miles south of Dublin, is a popular seaside resort in beautiful surroundings
Dun Laoghaire, à douze kilomètres au sud de Dublin, est une plage populaire entourée d'une ravissante campagne
Dun Laoghaire ist ein bekanntes, schöngelegenes Ferienbad etwa 12 km südlich von Dublin

Memorial Gardens alongside River Lee
Memorial Gardens, au bord de la Lee
Memorial Gardens am Lee

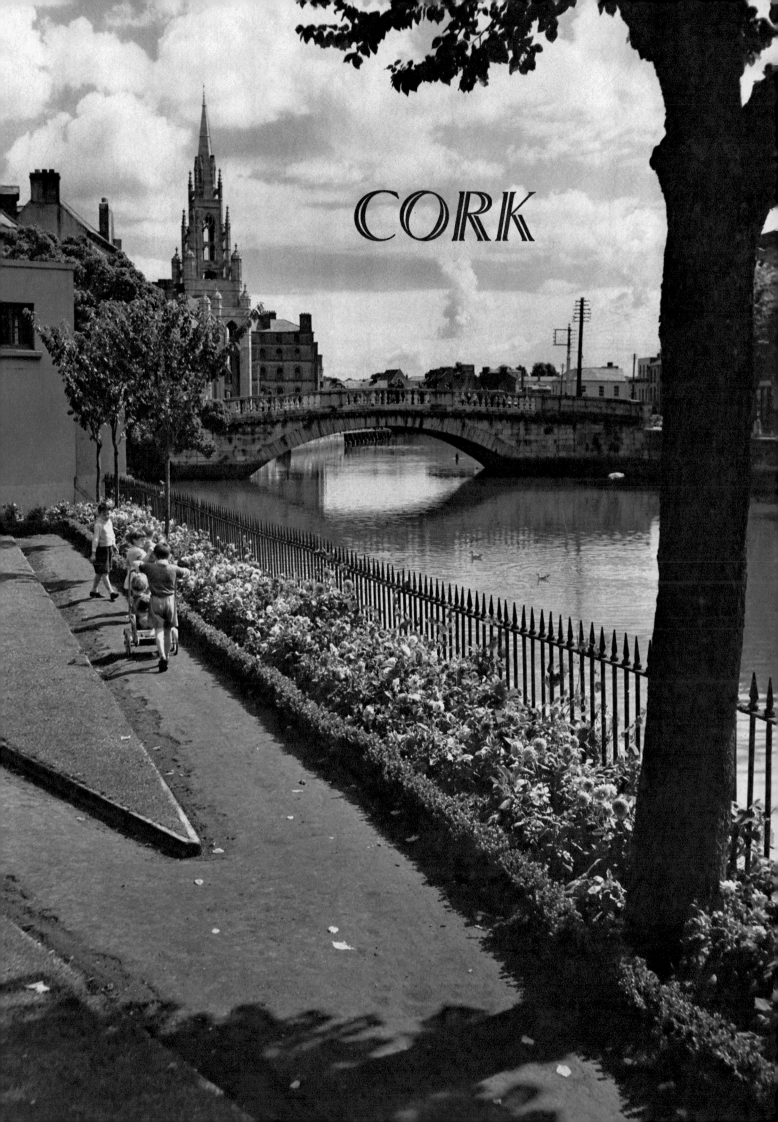

CORK

The Courthouse in Washington Street was restored after damage by fire during the political trials of 1891
Le palais de justice, Washington Street, a été restaurée après l'incendie qui l'endommagea lors des procès politiques de 1891
Das Gerichtsgebäude in der Washington Street brannte 1891 während der politischen Unruhen nieder und wurde wiederaufgebaut

The new Church of St. Francis in Liberty Street is built in the Byzantine style
La nouvelle église St. François, dans Liberty Street, conçue dans le style byzantin
Die neue Church of St. Francis in der Liberty Street wurde in byzantinischen Stil erbaut

The National Monument on Grand Parade was erected in memory of Irish patriots of the 19th century

Le Monument national, dans Grand Parade, a été érigé à la mémoire des patriotes irlandais du XIXème siècle

Das Nationaldenkmal auf der Grand Parade wurde zum Gedächtnis der irischen Patrioten des 19. Jahrhunderts errichtet

St. Patrick's Bridge, one of the many bridges spanning the River Lee
Le pont St. Patrick, l'un des nombreux ponts de la Lee
St. Patrick's Bridge, eine der vielen Brücken über den Lee

Market, Grand Parade
Le marché, Grand Parade
Markt auf der Grand Parade

Market, Cornmarket Street
Le marché, Cornmarket Street
Markt in der Cornmarket Street

Provincial Bank, South Mall

Morrison's Quay, with spire of Holy Trinity Church
Morrison's Quay, avec le clocher de la Sainte Trinité
Morrison's Quay mit dem Turm der Holy Trinity Church im Hintergrund

The new School of Commerce and Domestic Economy, Morrison's Quay
La nouvelle Ecole de commerce et de sciences domestiques, Morrison's Quay
Die neue Schule für Handel und Hauswirtschaft, Morrison's Quay

135

Statues of SS. Mark, Jude, Matthew and Peter on south portal of St. Fin Barre's
Statues de St. Marc, St. Jude, St. Mathieu et St. Pierre sur le portail sud de St. Fin Barre
Die Figuren der Apostel Markus, Judas, Matthäus und Petrus am Südeingang der St. Fin Barre's Cathedral

St. Fin Barre's Protestant Cathedral, from South Gate Bridge
La cathédrale protestante St. Fin Barre, vue de South Gate Bridge
Blick von der South Gate Bridge auf die protestantische St. Fin Barre's Cathedral

Augustinian Red Abbey, the Duke of Marlborough's headquarters during the siege of 1690

Augustinian Red Abbey, quartier général du duc de Marlborough pendant le siège de 1690

Augustinian Red Abbey: die Abtei diente dem Herzog von Marlborough während der Belagerung von 1690 als Hauptquartier

138

The bridge and gatehouse of University College
Le pont et la loge de garde, University College
Brücke und Pförtnerhaus des University College

139

University College, part of the National University: (Above) the attractive quadrangle: (right) the main gate
University College, partie de l'Université nationale. Ci-dessus : la belle cour carrée. A droite : l'entrée principale
University College, ein Teil der National University. Oben: der hübsche College-Hof, rechts: der Haupteingang

Fitzgerald Park: children's playground
Fitzgerald Park : au parc pour enfants
Fitzgerald Park: Kinderspielplatz

Fitzgerald Park: view of River Lee
Fitzgerald Park : vue sur la Lee
Fitzgerald Park: Blick auf den Lee

Franciscan monks
Moines franciscains
Franziskanermönche

Church of St. Vincent de Paul, Sunday's Well R

L'église St. Vincent de Paul, Sunday's Well R

Die Kirche St. Vincent de Paul an der Sund
Well Road

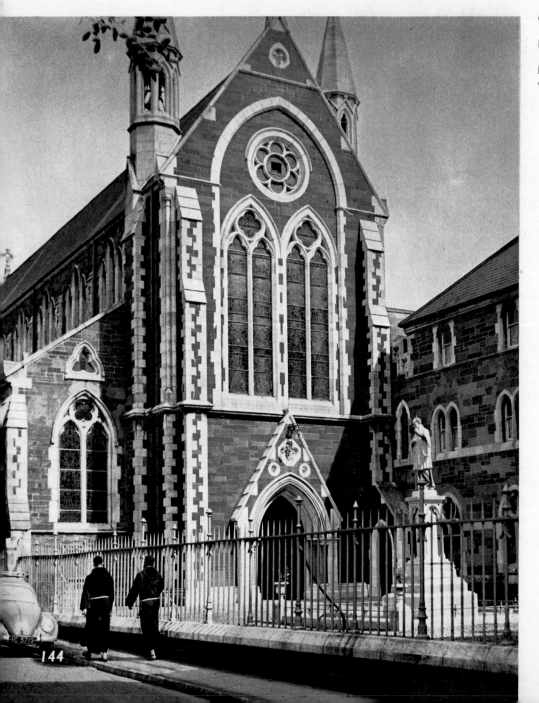

St. Fin Barre's, from Sunday's Well

St. Fin Barre, vue de Sunday's Well

Blick von der Sunday's Well Road auf St
Barre's Cath

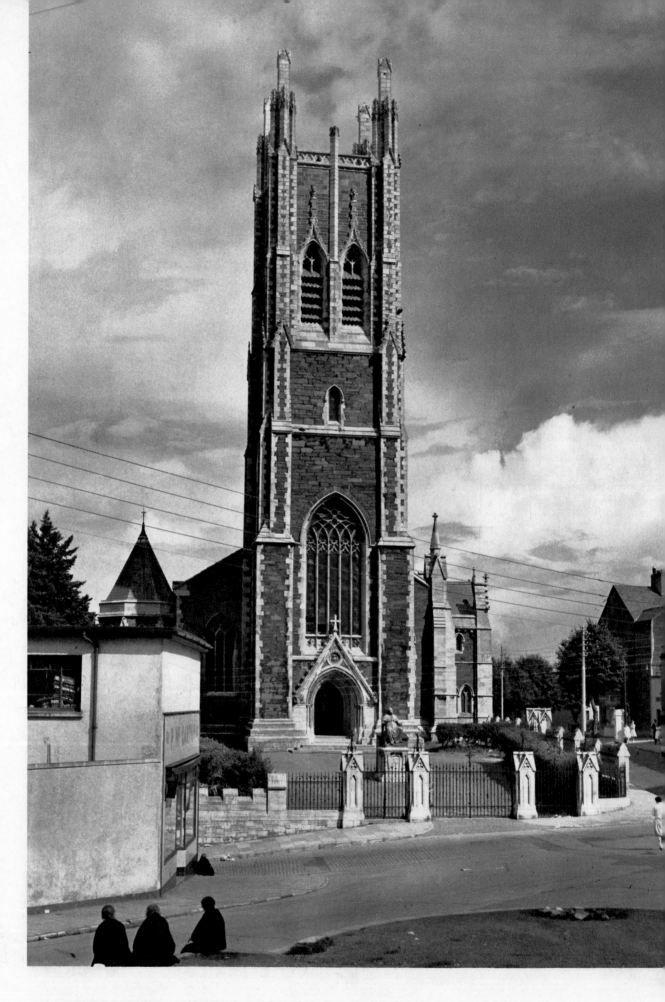

St. Mary's Roman Catholic Cathedral, Cathedral Street. The statue in front of the main entrance is of Bishop Delany
La cathédrale catholique Ste. Marie, Cathedral Street. La statue que l'on voit devant l'entrée est celle de l'évêque Delany
Die katholische St. Mary's Cathedral, Cathedral Street. Vor dem Haupteingang ein Standbild des Bischofs Delany

Tower of St. Ann's, Shandon. The steeple has two sides constructed of red sandstone and two of grey limestone
La tour de Ste. Anne, Shandon. La flèche a deux parois en grès rouge et deux en pierre à chaux grise
Turm der St. Ann's Church, Shandon: Zwei Seiten des Turmes sind aus rotem Sandstein, die anderen beiden aus grauem Kalkstein

The delicate spire of the Church of the Resurrection on Spangle Hill

Le délicat clocher de l'église de la Résurrection, Spangle Hill

Der grazile Turm der Church of the Resurrection im Vorort Spangle Hill

St. Mary's Dominican Church, Pope's Quay
L'église dominicaine Ste. Marie, Pope's Quay
Dominikanerkirche St. Mary's am Pope's Quay

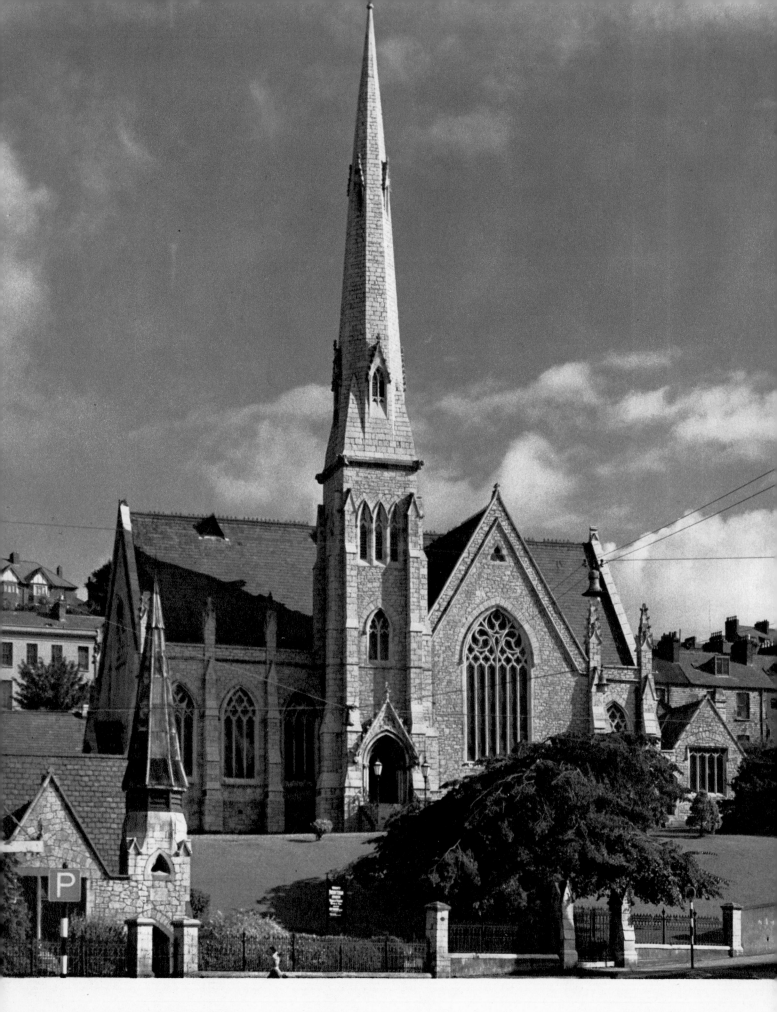

Presbyterian Church, Summer Hill
Eglise presbytérienne, Summer Hill
Presbyterianische Kirche in Summer Hill

Church of the Holy Trinity, or Father Mathew Memorial Church. The 'Apostle of Temperance' was superior here
L'église de la Ste. Trinité, également dédiée à «l'apôtre de la tempérance», le Père Mathew, qui y fut Supérieur
Church of the Holy Trinity, auch Father Mathew Memorial Church genannt. Dort war der 'Apostel der Mäßigung' Oberer

Cargo boat on River Lee. Cork, second only to Dublin in population, is likewise a flourishing port

Cargo sur la Lee. Cork, deuxième ville d'Irlande, est aussi un port florissant

Frachter auf dem Lee. Cork hat nach Dublin die größte Einwohnerzahl und ist unter anderem eine blühende Hafenstadt

Brian Boru Drawbridge. Brian Boru was the Irish king who finally defeated the Danes in 1014 and died on the battlefield
Brian Boru Drawbridge. Brian Boru est le roi irlandais qui trouva la mort en combattant victorieusement les Danois en 1014
Die Brian-Boru-Zugbrücke. Brian Boru war König der Iren; er besiegte die Dänen 1014 und fiel auf dem Schlachtfeld

The tower of City Hall framed by the drawbridge
La tour de l'Hôtel de Ville, encadrée par le pont à bascule
Turm der Stadthalle, eingerahmt von den Pfeilern der Zugbrücke

Offices of the Cork Steam Packet Company, Penrose's Quay
Bureaux de la Cork Steam Packet Company, Penrose's Quay
Bürohaus der Cork Steam Packet Company am Penrose's Quay

City Hall
L'Hôtel de Ville
Die Stadthalle

City Hall, seen from River Lee
L'Hôtel de Ville, vu des bords de la Lee
Blick von Lee auf die Stadthalle

Early morning, Albert Quay
Au petit matin, quai Albert
Frühmorgens am Albert Quay

Blackrock Castle, on a promontory outside the city, was designed originally for defensive purposes and is now a private residence

Blackrock Castle, érigé sur un promontoire, à l'entrée de la ville, fut construit à l'origine pour défendre la cité. C'est maintenant une demeure privée

Blackrock Castle: die Festung liegt auf einem Felsvorsprung außerhalb der Stadt; sie diente ursprünglich Verteidigungszwecken und ist heute ein privater Wohnsitz